The Low Countries

J.A. Kossmann-Putto & E.H. Kossmann

The Low Countries

History of the Northern and Southern Netherlands

Published by the
Flemish-Netherlands Foundation «Stichting Ons Erfdeel vzw»
1987

For a brief period in the nineteenth century, Belgium, the Netherlands and in a sense Luxemburg formed a political union in the Kingdom of the Netherlands, but this lasted for only fifteen years. Before this, these three had together sometimes formed part of a much larger empire as in the time of Charlemagne (born 742-died 814) and, ten centuries later, of Napoleon (1769-1821).

Before the end of the Middle Ages, no-one had attempted to subsume the whole region under one name. The term Low Countries (Lage Landen, Pays-Bas, Niederlande) originally referred very generally to the low-lying areas around the delta of the great rivers: Westphalia and the German Lower Rhineland were just as much part of it as the present-day Netherlands. This remained so until the fifteenth century and it was not until the sixteenth century that the term „Netherlands" acquired a more specific meaning: the region adjoining the North Sea whose various parts were under Habsburg rule. That said, however, the borders of these Low Countries were very different then from those of the present Benelux. In 1500, Holland and Zeeland in the north did indeed belong to the Low Countries, as did Brabant also, but the present-day provinces of Utrecht, Groningen, Friesland, Drenthe, Overijssel and part of Gelderland were only added in the course of the sixteenth century. Parts of Limburg remained outside until after the French Revolution, as did the large principality of Liège. Eupen and Malmédy were added in the twentieth century.

During the Middle Ages, after the disintegration of the Frankish kingdom in the ninth century, the fragmentation was very great. The bishops of Liège and Utrecht acquired secular power in parts of their diocese as a result of gifts from German kings, and they extended it by purchases and by wars. The other rulers took the opportunity of extending their power through marriage, which gave rise to combinations of „countries", some of a very temporary nature. Territory was also lost:

Artois, for example, which had in the past already had several changes of ruler, became part of France for good in 1659 together with a small part of Hainaut. France furthermore permanently acquired Dunkirk in 1662, Lille and its environs in 1668, Cambrai in 1678. Present-day Luxemburg is only the eastern part of the region over which the Dutch king William I became Grand-Duke in 1815; the west was incorporated in the brand new kingdom of Belgium in 1831 and in 1890 the east acquired its own grand-duke who was related to the Dutch royal house.

Economic unity was also absent from the territory covered by the Low Countries, although many parallel developments and many common interests can be discerned. Nor was there such a thing as cultural unity: Flanders, Brabant, Holland and Utrecht had been fairly closely connected for a long time, but in the Middle Ages the eastern provinces were strongly orientated towards Germany. Hainaut and Namur on the other hand showed a distinct orientation towards France with whom they, as was the case with part of Liège, shared a common language. The south of Brabant also belonged to the Romance language area. The political boundaries of modern times arose independently of these facts. The entities which came into being in the sixteenth century nevertheless gradually developed into modern self-contained states; the present Netherlands developing out of the federalist Republic of the Seven Provinces; and the Southern Netherlands, which were under foreign rule into the nineteenth century, giving rise to Belgium, which is now again displaying federalist tendencies, and, separate from it, Luxemburg.

2. Romans and Franks

When Julius Caesar subjected Gaul to Roman rule (58-51 BC) in a series of bloody wars as described by him in his famous book, *De Bello Gallico* (The Gallic War), he encountered tribes known collectively as the Belgae in this prosperous but politically divided region between the Seine and the Rhine. They gave their name to the Roman province of Gallia Belgica which was instituted some time after the conquest and divided into *civitates* - administrative districts which corresponded more or less to the regions inhabited by the various tribes. The population paid taxes to the Romans and provided troops for them. In the hundred years after Caesar's first conquest, the Romans also attempted to subjugate the (Germanic) region to the north and east of the Rhine. They gave this up after a time and this meant that the tribes living in what is now the Netherlands to the north of a line running through Nijmegen, Utrecht and Leiden, including the Frisians, were henceforth outside the borders of the empire and had only trade relations with the Romans.

In Gallia Belgica, however, the Romans set to work with great gusto, their main concern being military interests. Almost immediately, they began constructing an extensive network of roads and building army camps which rapidly attracted traders and craftsmen. After the conquest of Britain, Boulogne expanded into an important naval port. Land reforms made it possible to increase the grain harvest, which was of the utmost importance for feeding the enormous army concentrated in the North Sea region.

The Gallic aristocracy was clearly prepared to take on the administration of the *civitates* in the Roman empire with much the same leading role as before. They evidently had little difficulty in adapting to the Roman lifestyle, which was more comfortable and luxurious than they were accustomed to. At a lower level, the „Belgic" peasant population mixed with the newcomers, army veterans who had settled on land handed out to them to cultivate. The second century AD was a time when trade was flourishing and a local industry, having adopted all kinds of Roman techniques, was developing. From army camps and indigenous agglomerations, towns with a Roman

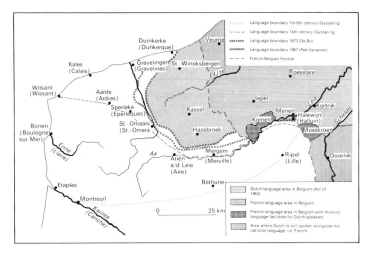

The shifting boundary between the Dutch-language and French-language areas.

appearance grew up: Tongeren, Nijmegen, Arlon, Tournai, Maastricht and others. A Gallo-Roman culture emerged with local variants. The Romans' influence, also on language usage, was strongest to the south of the great road which now linked Cologne with Bavai and Boulogne.

Towards the end of the third century, however, the empire weakened. This was due to internal circumstances, but also to devastating incursions by Germanic tribes into Gaul. Furthermore, a great deal of land along the coast and in the Rhine/Meuse/Scheldt delta which had once been inhabited, became a marshy, or even completely submerged, area. At the beginning of the fifth century, the Romans handed over the defence of the north to „Franks" who had already been allowed to settle in Texandria (Brabant) and who were now expanding their territory southwards. The establishment of the later linguistic boundary between Romance and Germanic in Belgium is closely bound up with this migration of peoples.

Shortly before 500, a Frankish chief from near Tournai put an end to Roman dominance over Gaul. By yet more victories and by the ruthless elimination of other Frankish kings, Clovis I expanded his territory in the south and east and founded a new kingdom, the Merovingian, and he took a very important step by being converted to Christianity. The Christianization of the region to the south of the great rivers, which had already begun under the Romans but had been interrupted by the Frankish incursions, was completed in the sixth and seventh centuries.

The Merovingian kings, whose kingdom stretched as far as the Pyrenees and far to the east of the Rhine, did not manage to secure internal order. The Franks did not have such a good grasp of abstract state institutions as their predecessors, the Romans. Under them, authority was a result of personal allegiances: of the notables to their king; of the free man to the lord to whose retinue he belonged; of the villein to the landowner to whose estate he was attached. It was a time of much internal unrest and great insecurity. Countless free farmers therefore renounced their privileged legal status and surrendered themselves and their small pieces of land to an influential man (or to an abbey) who was glad to lend them protection, knowing that in this way he was increasing not only his property but also his power. Sovereigns at this time had adapted the custom of rewarding their officials for their services by giving them land in fief which would give them an income in kind, the absence of an effective taxation system making the payment of salaries virtually impossible. In the centuries that followed, the system was expanded and refined, creating a network of personal relationships in which free men promised others allegiance and help, advice and service, and received in return land, possibly connected to an office, in fief, and a promise of equally loyal support. This was the so-called feudal system.

The Merovingian period was also a time of decivilization. The culture that the Romans had brought with them was for the most part lost, or was preserved and transmitted as best they could by small circles of people - in abbeys and at bishops' courts. In the eighth century, the Merovingians were pushed aside by the Carolingians who had grown powerful in their service. With the reign of Charlemagne (768-814), a time of florescence seemed for a while to have begun. After he had subjugated the Frisians and the Saxons in hard-fought campaigns, and at the same time had also forced them into officially adopting Christianity, he conducted a deliberate policy of reorganization and restoration. The kingdom was redivided into counties where an officer of the king, a count, represented his sovereign as judge and military commander. The restoration looked back to the Roman period. Charles had himself crowned Emperor by the Pope in Rome and attempted to halt the cultural decline by attracting scholars from Italy and Anglo-Saxon countries.

3. From the Ninth to the End of the Fourteenth Century

After Charles's death, much of what had only just been achieved was lost again, and the great Frankish empire disintegrated - including that part which now forms the Benelux. From then on, the boundary no longer ran along the great rivers. In the ninth century, almost all of Flanders became part of the West Frankish kingdom which later became France. From the tenth century, after a somewhat chaotic period, all the other „Netherlands" formed part of the German empire for a long time. On both sides of the boundary, however, the administrative districts developed into increasingly independent domains in which the counts - the erstwhile officials - worked their way up to be the rulers of virtually independent principalities, even though they were still bound by feudal ties to the French or German king. The boundary between east and west was of little importance for relations between these emergent countries. The fate of these small territories was determined by the endeavours of the rulers to increase their power and influence, by alliances of ruling houses, by disasters, diseases and infertility which affected the dynasties. A combination of such factors led in about 1300 to the union between Holland (with Zeeland and West Friesland) and Hainaut which had, at a previous stage, been attached to Flanders. Pure power politics on the part of the prince-bishops of Liège was rewarded with the expansion of their principality to include the county of Loon.

Although agriculture was the main means of existence, marked concentrations of industry and trade formed in the region of the rivers and along the coast. Trade was an important activity for the Frisians, even before they became part of the Frankish kingdom. In the eleventh century, the copper-beaters in the Meuse region were exporting their beautiful products to the Rhineland, and from the thirteenth century the towns along the IJssel took an active part in Hanseatic trade in the Baltic and North Sea regions. But all this was nothing compared with the flourishing cloth industry and international trade of Flanders and Brabant. In these areas, settlements of traders and craftsmen grew up into strong cities which were granted special rights by the counts and were therefore largely autonomous earlier than elsewhere in the Low Countries. In around 1340, Ghent was the largest city in Western Europe after Paris, and as much as a century before this, Bruges was attracting merchants from England, Italy and the Baltic.

Generally the cities were ruled by a magistracy constituted from an upper class of prosperous merchants. Here and there, the craftsmen who were united in guilds eventually also gained a share in the government. Both the wealth concentrated in the cities and their military strength gave the burghers influence outside their own city walls. The influence was greatest when the towns of a country determined their policies collectively, temporarily setting aside their day-to-day rivalries. So a count, duke or bishop who wanted to levy a special tax, or who was seeking support for his dynastic or foreign policies, called to-

The 12th-century baptismal font in the Church of St. Bartholomew, Liège, a prime example of the art of copper chasing in the Meuse region.

gether not only the most eminent nobles and prelates in his country, but also representatives of the towns in order to gain their co-operation. It was not unusual for certain favours and privileges to be requested in return. In the course of the late Middle Ages, the so-called States Assemblies evolved from these consultations, with the three classes or „states" representing church, nobility and citizenry. And yet the ruler came into conflict often enough with his towns, or with one town, and this easily gave rise to small internal wars. In Flanders, these struggles were repeatedly complicated by the interference of the French king as the Flemish counts' feudal lord. The Flemish citizens were in general anti-French. Citizen armies won fame by defeating a splendid army of French and Flemish knights in the Battle of the Golden Spurs (1302). For the sake of Flemish wool imports, folk heroes like Jacob and Philip van Artevelde pursued strongly pro-English policies, much to the displeasure of the French king and in spite of the feudal relationship between Flanders and France. The history of the northern Netherlands in the Middle Ages also has its heroes but they were not burghers: Witte van Haemstede, who helped repel a Flemish incursion, was a bastard of the house of the counts of Holland; Jan van Schaffelaar, who met his death during a siege in Holland, was a third-rate condottiere.

4. The Increasing Power of the Dukes of Burgundy

Flanders proceeded with its pro-English policy even after it had passed to the Duke of Burgundy, youngest son of the French king, through his marriage in 1363. The latter's grandson Philip the Good (1396-1467), efficient and ambitious, continued this policy with conviction. He furthermore made himself master of the Holland/Hainaut complex of territories through his involvement in internal affairs, and also of Brabant (a duchy with an important textile industry and with considerable political influence to the north and east of the great rivers), Namur and Luxemburg. He owed his nickname to the concern he showed for the Flemish economy and the emergent economy of Holland.

The lifestyle of the Burgundian dukes was different from that of the sovereigns who had preceded them in the Netherlands: it vied with that of the French court where most of them had grown up, and their princely airs gave the culture of the Netherlands a powerful boost. It had flourished at times during the preceding centuries. Under Bishop Notker (c. 1000), who

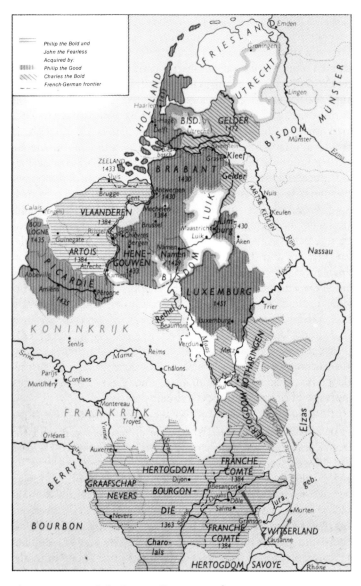

The emergence of the Burgundian monarchy.

came to the north from the Abbey of Sankt Gallen, Liège became a centre of learning where in addition to theological and philosophical problems, mathematics and questions of music theory were studied. In the „renaissance of the twelfth century" Alanus de Insulis (Alain de Lille), poet and philosopher, occupied an eminent position. He wrote in Latin, the normal written language of his time which was to remain the medium of scholarship for centuries. However, poems in French and Dutch have survived even from this century. Architecture followed the great Romanesque and Gothic traditions in France and Germany with imposing cathedrals and abbeys, and the citizens in the big towns paraded their wealth in their town halls, market halls and gateways. The Burgundians did, however, introduce a new element into cultural life: a court culture in the French style. By their commissions, they stimulated painters and sculptors who were evolving a new genre at this period (so-called Flemish Primitivism) and in whose work the representation of people and landscape had a realistic, secular character. Both Claus Sluter from Haarlem, famed for his „Well of Moses" in the monastery of Champmol near Dijon, and Jan van Eyck, painter of the equally famous Ghent altarpiece, the „Adoration of the Lamb", and admired for his portraiture, were in the service of the court. Poets and chroniclers also found inspiration here, and there was never any shortage of harmonic modern music.

The primary purpose of the splendour and luxury of the court was a political one: to put the dukes on a par with the French king; to impress the leading citizens for whom wealth and power were anyhow synonymous; to lure the elite of nobles who were keen to become associated with the sovereign through taking on important offices. The backbone of what was to grow into a cohesive Burgundian state was formed by a tightly-knit group of officials, lawyers and financial experts. Philip the Good and Charles the Bold (1433-1477) did not only dream of a „kingdom of Friesland" stretching from the

Wadden Sea to Burgundy: they also geared their policies to its realization. Charles the Bold had a conscious policy of expansion which cost his Netherlands subjects a great deal of money, and he modernized the administration in the Low Countries by setting up a central exchequer in Lille and a high court for all the provinces, the so-called Parliament of Mechelen. These were unpopular measures, which were nevertheless adopted. But the duke did not achieve his aim. He fell in battle in 1477 near Nancy fighting against the troops of the Swiss Confederation and the Lotharingians, while attempting to maintain his rule over Alsace/Lorraine which he had acquired previously and which was now being challenged.

The king of France, Louis XI (1423-1483), who had long been his bitter enemy, benefitted from the disorganization of the Burgundian empire by returning its heartland, Burgundy itself, to the French crown as a lapsed fief and by attacking the Low Countries. Although they did not rejoice over Charles's death, the provinces of the Netherlands benefitted from it by forcing Mary, Charles's twenty-year-old daughter (1457-1482), to make far-reaching concessions which they stipulated as the condition for their support for her in the struggle against France and which restored their independence of the central government. The German imperial house, the Habsburgs, also profited from it. With the permission of the States-General of the Netherlands provinces, the son of emperor Frederick III, Maximilian of Austria (1459-1519), married Mary who had been promised to him in earlier years before the emperor had joined Charles's opponents. To the Habsburgs, the marriage meant a considerable expansion of the family possessions, even though they had to relinquish Burgundy, and Maximilian had to bring all his power to bear to keep the Netherlands out of Louis XI's hands.

At first he had to be content with an unfavourable peace which had been forced on him by the Netherlands States-

General after the unexpected death of Mary in 1482. Maximilian's position was very difficult at that time. Mary's son Philip (1478-1506) was much too young to rule, but the States-General were not inclined to put his father in a strong position as regent. Furthermore, immediately after Mary's death there was unrest throughout the territory. At first, Maximilian had his hands full intervening in civil wars in Holland and in Utrecht, where the power of a bishop and ally, David of Burgundy (d. 1496), was at stake. After this, in the south, serious disturbances broke out when Maximilian resumed the war with France to win back the territories he had ceded. Flanders wanted peace and received the support of a large number of Netherlanders. This resulted in a war against Maximilian which lasted for years and brought much misery to the population of the southern Netherlands and in the end produced nothing for the rebels. A skilful diplomatic manœuvre enabled Maximilian to restore order and he actually recovered the regions lost in 1482, including Artois.

In 1493 Maximilian succeeded his father as ruler of the German empire and a year later, Philip the Fair was declared of age. He was a cautious politician. He refused to confirm the Great Privilege granted by his mother in 1477 to the States-General and revived the high court in Mechelen, but in his foreign policy he avoided taking an explicitly pro-French or pro-English line. He has been praised for having a „Netherlands" policy, not geared towards dynastic interests like that of his father. But he could only adopt such a policy because Maximilian had worked hard at preserving the southern provinces as an integral part of the Burgundian empire and at guarding Flanders against the danger of being drawn into the French sphere of influence.

Philip's marriage to Joan of Aragon (1479-1554), daughter of the Spanish king, was of great importance for the Habsburg dynasty: in 1504 she unexpectedly succeeded her

The marriage of Maximilian of Habsburg and Mary of Burgundy in 1477. In the course of the 16th century the Habsburg dynasty, which at this time already ruled part of Southern Germany and the whole of Austria, acquired Spain, Southern Italy, Bohemia and part of Hungary. In 1522 it split into an Austrian and a Spanish branch.

mother the Queen of Castile as the latter's only surviving heir. Philip himself died shortly afterwards, but when Joan's father, King Ferdinand of Aragon also died in 1516, the whole of Spain with its rich American colonies fell to her eldest son, Charles V, born in Ghent in 1500, lord of the Netherlands since 1506, and since 1519, as Maximilian's successor, Emperor of Germany.

5. Emperor Charles V, Ruler of the Netherlands

According to school book tradition, the Modern Period began for the Netherlands with Charles V (1500-1558). There were some grounds for dividing history up in this way, although nowadays it is more usual to emphasize the continuity of late fifteenth-century and early sixteenth-century developments. Humanism - an intellectual movement which originated in Italy and aimed to continue the culture of classical antiquity, rejecting medieval scholastic philosophy - was flourishing. Its most significant representative in the Netherlands was Erasmus of Rotterdam, witty man of letters, learned philologist and incisive theologian, who gave a pedagogical meaning to all his work: that of education towards a purer morality and a more civilized existence. He shared this emphasis on the significance of education and a straightforward biblical Christianity with rational features with the circle called the Modern Devotion, from which he himself had emerged. Later on, around 1540, the influence of the Renaissance penetrated into civic architecture and into sculpture.

Around 1500, the economy of the Low Countries entered a period of powerful expansion which was promoted by the rise of the Habsburg empire. Between 1495 and 1520, Antwerp became the largest metropolis for trade in the west, a centre for European transit trade and a port through which goods from the Spanish colonies in America and the Portuguese colonies in West Africa were imported. The traditional textile

19

industry was doing badly, but all kinds of highly specialized small industries were thriving: bell-founding, tapestry, book printing. However, the constantly fluctuating grain prices and the inflation which was caused in the early decades by the population increase and by American gold and silver pouring into Europe, had grave consequences for the masses. Begging, which had already begun to assume disturbing proportions in the course of the fifteenth century, now had to be countered by the authorities with powerful general measures.

Charles V's Netherlands policy resembled, in essence, that of his forbear Charles the Bold. It was expansionist and was geared towards an efficient, somewhat centralized government. The Habsburg Netherlands acquired new borders. The secular territory of the Bishop of Utrecht, Friesland, Groningerland, the dukedom of Gelre and in the south the episcopal city of Tournai and environs were added to Charles's state in the first half of the sixteenth century. The feudal ties which bound Flanders and Artois to the French king were severed with the Treaty of Cambrai in 1529. These provinces were now included in the German empire, but after 1548 together with the rest of the Habsburg Netherlands, they formed the so-called Burgundian Kreis (Circle), which was linked very loosely to the government of the empire. As emperor, Charles V never for one moment neglected the interests of his house.

Charles's government was, in the Burgundian tradition, geared towards centralization of governmental power. In practice, however, he often had to hand over to a representative. First his aunt acted as regent and circumstances forced her to make a fair number of concessions to the demands of the provincial States. In 1530 she was succeeded by a sister of the emperor's. The new regent was supported by a totally new government organization, instituted by Charles himself in a year when he was residing almost constantly in Brussels.

A Council of State was created with the most eminent nobles as members. The intention was to bind these lords more closely to the sovereign's policies. Alongside this, however, was a Secret Council, consisting of skilled lawyers with modern views on the role of the sovereign and the nature of the state, and with little sympathy for individual provinces' desire for independence. This council was given wide powers. A Council of Finance completed the organization. At the same time, Charles promulgated a series of measures, applicable to the entire Netherlands, dealing with, amongst other things, the care of the poor.

Although Charles V had achieved a great deal, he did not look back on the results of his efforts with satisfaction when he abdicated in 1555. The unity of the Netherlands so desired by him was threatened by the profound differences of opinion about the doctrine and organization of the Church which are encapsulated in the term Reformation. The theology of Luther, and later on Calvin, the theories of the Anabaptists with their revolutionary tendencies spread quite rapidly amongst the urban population of Brabant and Flanders, Holland and Zeeland. The strong measures promulgated against all forms of Protestantism were to no avail. Instead, they reinforced the displeasure of local authorities who saw them as a restriction on their own jurisdiction, which they already regarded as threatened by various centralizing measures.

6. The Eighty Years' War

The social, economic, political and religious tensions came to a head under Philip II (1556-1598), who succeeded his father as King of Spain and Lord of the Netherlands. Philip had been educated in Spain and did not know the Low Countries well; after 1559 he never visited them again. An earnest man with honourable intentions, he wanted to continue Charles V's policies and uphold both the authority of the monarchy and that of the Roman Catholic Church in their full splendour. His

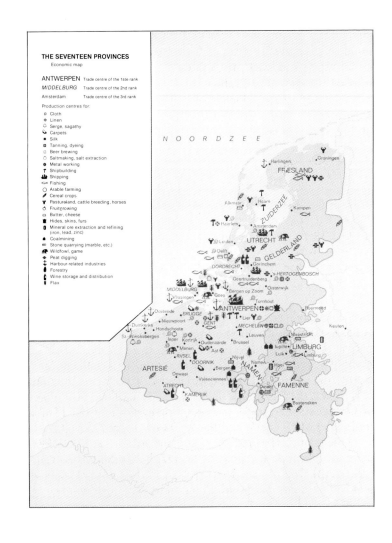

The economic situation in the Low Countries around 1559.

government of the Netherlands turned into a disaster. The flood of „heresies", by now mostly Calvinist in nature, could no longer be stemmed. An economic depression hit the industries of Flanders and Brabant and contributed to the king's financial difficulties, which eventually ended in bankruptcy. A reorganization of the tax system, which was still based on each of the various provincial States giving its consent, was a matter of urgency from the government's point of view, but proved unacceptable to the people.

It was at the highest level that the opposition first took concrete shape. The most prominent noblemen, who represented the sovereign as stadholders in the different provinces but whose influence on the policies adopted in Brussels was negligible, were well aware of the widespread discontent among the population. Led by Prince William of Orange (1533-1584), who was stadholder of Holland, Zeeland and Utrecht and owned vast estates in Brabant, they formed the League of Noblemen and tried to persuade the king to change his internal policies. Soon, however, the differences intensified and the initiative to resist passed to other groups. In 1566 the Calvinists forcibly seized church buildings in a number of villages and towns (the so-called Iconoclastic Riots). Two years later the new regent, the Duke of Alva (1507-1582), had two of William of Orange's supporters - the Count of Egmond (1522-1568), stadholder of Flanders, and the Count of Horne (1524-1568), stadholder of Gelderland - arrested and beheaded. With their dramatic execution the Duke of Alva set about the task entrusted to him: that of crushing every sign of Protestantism and opposition. Their deaths are also traditionally seen as marking the beginning of the Revolt of the Netherlands, the „Eighty Years' War".

In the first few years events moved quickly. A fleet of Protestant refugees who were roaming the seas as privateers (the so-called Sea Beggars) captured the port of Den Briel, in southern Holland, in 1572. The provinces of Holland and Zeeland then rebelled, and from that moment onwards the attempts by the Spanish king to beat the whole of the Low Countries into submission proved in vain. The other provinces joined the revolt against Philip II in 1576, but in 1579 some of the southern territories, including Hainaut and Artois, formed the Union of Arras, accepting the authority of the king and the Roman Catholic Church. Shortly afterwards most of the remaining provinces signed the Union of Utrecht, declaring in 1581 that they no longer recognized the King as their sovereign. Not all of these regions were able to maintain their independence. Flanders and Brabant were reconquered by Spanish troops after a few years. The others remained united, and from the end of the century onwards they constituted the Republic of the United Netherlands.

Thus the Revolt of the Netherlands ultimately led to the secession of the northern provinces from the Spanish empire and to the creation of a new, autonomous state. In fact, this was not what the rebels had consciously set out to accomplish. Calvinism had become firmly established in the South well before it proved successful in Holland and Zeeland. The economic depression of around 1550, which had caused so much discontent, had affected the South more gravely than it had the North. The political opposition had originally been concentrated in Brussels. Independence of the Spanish crown was certainly not the objective from the start, and William of Orange, the great leader, only resigned himself in the last few years of his life (he was murdered in 1584 by a supporter of the Spanish king) to the fact that the territory which had been united under Charles V would be divided into two parts.

The Union of Arras and the subsequent Spanish reconquests resulted in a religious as well as a political separation. For the South this meant that the people, whether they had taken sides in the religious disputes out of conviction or had occupied the middle ground, were obliged to adopt the Roman Catholic faith of the Counter-Reformation. For the North it meant that Calvinism was now the officially accepted religion, and other forms of religious practice were hedged around with all kinds of restrictions. The ideal of different denominations peacefully co-existing, which had been so dear to William of Orange, proved impossible to achieve in the sixteenth century.

On the whole, neither the North nor the South was prepared to acquiesce in the division of the Low Countries, but in the seventeenth century it became clear that the obstacles to reunification were insurmountable. The North, where the Protestants did not constitute the majority of the population but nevertheless held political power until the end of the Republic, lost interest in the Southern provinces as the latter returned to the Catholic fold. Moreover, the North no longer needed the South, for its own economy was going through a remarkable development. When in 1585 Antwerp, the last stronghold of the United Provinces in the South, was forced to surrender to the Spanish regent, the Duke of Parma, the rebels lost their largest and richest mercantile city. But it was soon apparent that other towns, Amsterdam foremost among them, were able to replace Antwerp. The exodus of tens of thousands of Calvinists from what were now the Spanish Netherlands proved to be of great benefit to the North. The Flemings and Brabanters shared with the Hollanders their specialized economic know-how, they brought their capital and international commercial contacts, and they contributed much to the spectacular growth of Amsterdam, which saw its population double in size between 1600 and 1620 and then increase still further to approximately 150,000 around 1650.

In the South, the damage was directly proportional to this success. Whereas around 1560 Antwerp had some 100,000 inhabitants, by 1589 there were a mere 42,000 left. By

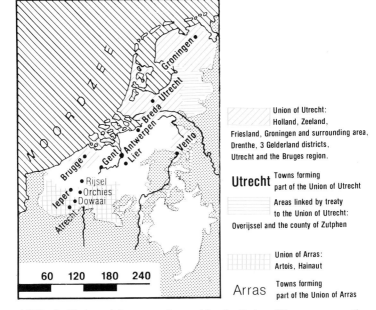

1579: the Union of Arras, engineered by the Duke of Parma, reconciled Artois and Hainaut with Spain; the Union of Utrecht was established by Count John of Nassau (brother of William the Silent) to co-ordinate resistance to Spanish military power. Note: Luxemburg had no part in the Revolt.

blockading the mouth of the river Scheldt the Northern provinces prevented direct access to the port from the North Sea. Although after a time it recovered somewhat and acquired an important role as a link between the Spanish part of the world and a Dutch Republic not averse to some profitable trading with the enemy, the city had lost its dominant place in international commerce. Agriculture again took a larger share in the Southern economy, and new industries emerged in the countryside: lace-making, nail-manufacture, and also linen-weaving, which turned Kortrijk (Courtrai) into an important linen market. The situation, then, was not as catastrophic as it has sometimes been made out to be, but compared with the region's former prosperity and the new ascendancy of Holland, there was little reason for satisfaction.

The economic expansion of Holland and Zeeland gave the Republic a political impetus which no-one could have predicted when at the end of the 1580s the provincial States declared themselves the bearers of sovereignty within their own borders. Of the seven provinces, Holland was far and away the most important, the wealthiest and the most populous, an economic and cultural focus of international significance. This preponderance was not constitutionally laid down. The Republic was a federal state, governed by the States-General, which consisted of representatives of the seven provinces recognized as members. The territories which the Republic recovered from Spain after the fall of Antwerp were accorded a different status: they were administered as „lands of the Generality" until the end of the Republic and had no voice in the decision-making process. From the end of the sixteenth century onwards the States-General met permanently in The Hague. Each province had one vote, so in theory Holland and the other provinces were equals. The States-General looked after the Republic's external interests: they decided on war and peace, and concluded treaties with foreign powers. When early in the seventeenth century two large companies were established with a view to organizing the emerging trade with Asia (United East India Company, 1602) and America (West India Company, 1621), they received their monopolies from the States-General, who also appointed their boards of directors, the „governors". The „Generality" itself had virtually no direct source of revenue. In all matters of importance the members of the States-General were obliged to reach unanimous decisions. They were bound by the instructions of their provincial authorities and had to consult with them whenever problems arose unforeseen.

The real power, then, lay with the provincial States. In Gelderland and Overijssel, in Friesland and Groningen, the nobility played a more prominent part than it did in Holland, in whose States the towns had eighteen delegates and the nobility just one. The role of the provincial States had not been without importance in the later Middle Ages. In theory at least they could grant or refuse the levying of special taxes, and in times of doubtful hereditary succession their preference determined who would hold power as count, duke or prince-bishop. But apart from these so-called „privileges" their role was merely advisory, and they met only at the request of the sovereign. From the end of the sixteenth century onwards, however, they themselves constituted the highest authority in their respective regions, an authority which had previously been vested in the sovereign. They consequently appointed the stadholder (the representative of the sovereign). In the first years of the Revolt the provinces of Holland, Zeeland and Utrecht recognized as their stadholder William of Orange, who had been dismissed from that office by Philip II. Later it became customary for all provinces, except those in the north of the Republic, to appoint one of William of Orange's descendants as their stadholder, while Groningen and Friesland opted for a member of a related branch of the House of Nassau. In other respects, too, the provincial States exercised all the rights belonging to a monarch: they decided on the imposition of taxes and enacted those laws which were of more than purely local scope. And through their delegates in the States-General they had a say in the government of the Republic.

The stadholders of the two northern provinces did not much involve themselves in national or international affairs. For their colleague who represented the other five provinces it was a very different matter. His position contained a certain ambiguity in that his powers of government derived from the regional authorities, but it was the States-General who appointed him supreme commander of the army and navy. Prince

William had not been a military genius, but his son Maurice (1567-1625) was. Having made a thorough study of the writings on strategy and tactics of classical antiquity (with the assistance of the Humanist scholar Justus Lipsius), and helped by the mathematical expertise of Simon Stevin, he modernized military strategy. Together with his cousin William Louis, stadholder of Friesland, Maurice succeeded in securing for the Republic the entire area north of the great rivers.

The Twelve Years' Truce (1609-1621) provided a breathing-space. When it ended Maurice's younger brother Frederick Henry (1584-1647) assumed command of the army, which now enjoyed international renown as a training-school for the art of war. He added northern Brabant and parts of Zeeland-Flanders and Limburg to the territory of the Republic, but failed in his attempts to recapture Antwerp. His military successes and the country's general prosperity enabled Frederick Henry to cultivate, in a modest way, a royal court style, which suited him as sovereign of the independent principality of Orange. He acquired a royal bride, a daughter of Charles I of England, for his son William II (1626-1650). With this marriage the House of Orange and the English throne entered into a lasting relationship.

The Southern Netherlands remained in Spanish hands until 1700. In 1598 Philip II bequeathed the territory as a „fief of the Spanish crown" to his daughter Isabella (1566-1633) and her husband Archduke Albert of Austria (1559-1621), thus granting it a semblance of autonomy, which disappeared when the region returned to Spain upon Isabella's death. The governmental institutions from the days of Charles V remained in place. In the seventeenth century a Council of Flanders came into being; it was based in Madrid and charged, among other things, with supervision of the Council of Finance. The high nobility lost much of its influence after the Revolt, one reason being that the powers of the office of stadholder were severely

Rombout Verhulst (Mechelen 1624-1698), terracotta model of the tomb of the naval hero Maarten Harpertsz. Tromp (killed at sea in 1653), part of the mausoleum in Delft.

curtailed. The regional States, however, retained their traditional rights. Their consent was required when the sovereign wanted to change local institutions or levy extra taxes. The stadholders also sought their advice in purely administrative matters, so that their influence steadily grew. The States-General, on the other hand, were rarely convened under Albert and Isabella, and after 1632 they never assembled again.

7. The Peace That Did Not Bring Peace

The war between Spain and the Dutch Republic ended with the Peace of Munster in 1648. Spain was obliged to recognize the Republic's independence, and the ties between the United Provinces and the German Empire were severed. The peace treaty, far from heralding a period of calm, marked the beginning of a new era in international relations, one in which

Spain no longer played a significant part. The autonomy of the Spanish Netherlands was now threatened, not by the Republic, as had been the case in the 1630s, but by France. The new state of affairs was confirmed in the Treaty of the Pyrenees (1659), as a result of which Artois was lost for good. Shortly afterwards the French king Louis XIV made another attempt to annex the Spanish Netherlands, but the Republic, not keen to have a powerful and aggressive France as its neighbour, managed to prevent this by diplomatic means.

In the years following the Peace of Munster the Republic had tried to maintain the international balance of power through the use of diplomacy. However, increasing friction between the princes of Orange - first Frederick Henry, then William II - and the regent class of Holland concerning the wisdom of this policy, together with pressing questions of war and peace and the strength of the armed forces, finally resulted, after William II's death, in the decision by a majority of provinces not to appoint another stadholder in 1650. The republican idea, supported wholeheartedly by the regents of Holland and their Grand Pensionary Johan de Witt, reigned supreme. The aim was to adopt a cautious foreign policy, as neutral as possible, and to grant the largest possible measure of autonomy to the individual regions. In practice it meant that, although wars were fought almost without interruption during the 1650s and '60s, their sole purpose was to defend the commercial interests of the maritime provinces and of the big trading companies in the Far East and America against English competition and the Swedish threat to free navigation in the Baltic. They were all naval wars. The Dutch admirals - Maarten Tromp, Michiel de Ruyter - were celebrated as national heroes and honoured with splendid monuments after their deaths.

The Republic was in this period one of the great powers of Europe, with a thriving economy, based on Holland's trade, and a remarkably high level of culture. The range of cultural

The Low Countries after the Peace of Munster (1648).

NOORDZEE

GRONINGEN
Leeuwarden Groningen

FRIESLAND

DRENTHE

Zwolle

OVERIJSSEL

HOLLAND Amsterdam

UTRECHT Zutphen
Utrecht GELDERLAND

Rotterdam

Munster

HEILIG

ZEELAND 's Hertogenbosch
NOORD-BRABANT

Middelburg

ROOMSE

RIJK

Brugge Antwerpen
Duinkerke Gent Mechelen
VLAANDEREN BRABANT Keulen
Ieper Leuven Maastricht
Brussel Sint-Truiden
Doornik Luik LIMBURG
Bergen Namen
ARTESIË NAMEN Stavelot
Atrecht HENEGOUWEN Stavelot
Kamerijk

Bouillon LUXEMBURG
FRANKRIJK Luxemburg Trier

0 km 75

The Dutch Republic

The Spanish Netherlands

The Principality of Liège, etc.

Present-day national frontiers

expression was most striking. We know the names of the great painters: Rembrandt, Vermeer, Jan Steen, Frans Hals and many others. The character of Dutch art was determined in part by the fact that the Republic lacked two types of patronage which were of crucial importance in other countries: a royal court and a church fond of ostentation. The Spanish South did have this kind of patronage, and it showed in the work of its leading artists, Rubens and Van Dyck. In the Republic, orders for large-scale works of art came from private individuals and especially from the town councils; Amsterdam's town hall is the most impressive example in this respect, both as an architectural feat and on account of its internal decoration. The ample opportunities to undertake work of this nature attracted numerous Southern architects and sculptors to the Republic during the seventeenth century.

Could Dutch literature boast comparable successes? P.C. Hooft, Joost van den Vondel and Constantijn Huygens were certainly acknowledged as being of the first order, and profusely honoured in their own country both during their lifetimes and by later generations. But in contrast with the great contemporary painters, they were hardly known or read outside the Netherlands, not even in translation. The fame of the scholars and scientists, however, spread far and wide. Hugo de Groot (or Grotius) is internationally regarded as a jurist of seminal importance. Christiaan Huygens and Jan Swammerdam ranked among the foremost scientists of their time. Even though in the seventeenth century only a fairly small circle was able to grasp Spinoza's philosophy, from the eighteenth century onwards the most advanced writers and thinkers throughout Europe treated his work with the utmost respect. It is not surprising that foreign intellectuals who felt threatened in their own countries, found in the Republic a place that afforded relative peace and freedom and where they had an audience: Descartes, Locke, Pierre Bayle and many others came to live and work for longer or shorter periods in this remarkable country.

The self-confidence characteristic of the Republic around 1650 was abruptly shattered when Louis XIV, still intent on conquering the Spanish Netherlands, struck an alliance with England, declared war on the United Provinces in 1672 and swiftly occupied a sizeable part of the country. William II's son, also called William, who until then had been excluded from all public offices, was hurriedly appointed army commander and stadholder. After William III had warded off the danger, the regents were at first reluctant to continue the resolutely anti-French policies he advocated, but they changed their minds when in 1685 Louis XIV revoked the Edict of Nantes (which had granted French Protestants a degree of protection) and James II, a Roman Catholic convert, became King of England. The Republic fully supported William III, who was married to James II's daughter Mary Stuart, when in 1688 he joined forces with the English Protestants and drove out his father-in-law. The „Glorious Revolution" put the Dutch stadholder, the servant of the States-General, on the English throne and closely tied the United Provinces to English politics.

In the last quarter of the century the Spanish Netherlands were ravaged by French military campaigns, which culminated in 1678 in the capture of Ypres and Ghent. The long years of intermittent war and peace took a turn for the worse when in 1700 the Spanish Habsburg dynasty died out with Charles II and confusion over his succession rendered the future of the Southern Netherlands very uncertain. Louis XIV claimed the entire Spanish inheritance for his grandson, the German Emperor did the same on behalf of one of his sons. Several European countries became embroiled in the War of the Spanish Succession (1701-1714), which resulted in the Southern Netherlands coming under the sovereignty of the Austrian branch of the House of Habsburg. The Republic continued to exercise its right to maintain garrisons in a number of Southern towns as a safeguard against renewed French aggression. But the garrisons were poorly equipped and proved worthless when a new war of succession (1740-1748) broke out.

The principality of Liège steered clear of these wars. It was exceptional in other respects too. The bishops, who were elected, were accountable to a complicated system of representative bodies and had little power. The principality thus enjoyed greater intellectual freedom than the rest of the Southern Netherlands. Its economy was less dependent on agriculture than was the case in neighbouring regions, and it had a stronger manufacturing base. The arms industry was of international importance, and Liège nails, used in shipbuilding, found a ready market in the Republic. Liège also benefitted from the fact that it was exempt from the various restrictions imposed by the Republic on trade with countries under Habsburg rule. In the course of the eighteenth century its manufacturing industry grew in size and became more modern.

In the Southern Netherlands of the early eighteenth century the cottage industries that had developed some time before, still predominated. English and Dutch opposition prevented the growth of overseas trade, and the coal industry was unable to expand because the mines in Hainaut and Namur were still owned by abbeys or by the nobility. But the population increased sharply, and towards the end of the century Flanders and Brabant witnessed the emergence of a new cotton-based textile industry which from the start bore a modern, capitalist stamp. The Austrian authorities promoted industrial development, although their efforts were not always successful. In the second half of the century they adopted an enlightened policy, allowing the Southern Netherlands more intellectual freedom than they had been used to for a long time. But the Enlightenment reached only the French-speaking part of the population. This group was growing larger in the Dutch-language region in this period because the nobility and the upper middle classes came to regard French as the cultured language *par excellence*. French was also used in those ecclesiastical circles that were beginning to resist the influx of enlightened ideas. The Dutch language thus acquired a mark of social inferiority.

The Republic had become receptive to the Enlightenment at an early stage. Its ideas dominated Dutch eighteenth-century culture, which, taking its cue largely from France, was very refined but somewhat less colourful than it had been in the seventeenth century. After the War of the Spanish Succession the United Provinces had lost their position as a great power on the European political scene. They no longer took any initiatives that might have caused upheaval. When William III died childless, several provinces opted for a second stadholderless period. The policy of neutrality favoured by the regent classes of Holland and Zeeland could be continued undisturbed until 1747, when France was poised once more to invade the Republic in the War of the Austrian Succession. Orangists in Holland and Zeeland, supported by a large section of the population, demanded the restoration of the stadholderate, and William IV of Orange (1711-1751), a distant cousin of William III and stadholder of Friesland, Groningen, Drenthe and Gelderland, now became the first stadholder of all the United Provinces. The position of the Republic, however, did not change appreciably, partly also because after years of neglect the army and navy were ill prepared for an active international role.

The economic situation was less gloomy, but in this field too the Republic lost its former prominence, though not so much through inactivity as through a lack of foreign demand for the services offered by the Dutch. Holland ceased to be a staple market for grain from the Baltic and raw materials, and the volume of its trade no longer increased because of the growing economic power of England in particular. Manufacturing industry, too, found fewer new outlets. Competition on the international market was hampered by the Republic's exceptionally high level of wages.

The ruling class of Holland, the „regents", who were very much involved in trade and industry in the first half of the seventeenth century, had gradually withdrawn from that sphere. They preferred to invest their capital in landed estates and in bonds, and occupied administrative posts at local, provincial and national level. Their colleagues in the agrarian regions were an equally exclusive caste. The families from which they came could be divided into two „parties", which exercised power alternately: Orangists on the one hand, and those who were opposed to the stadholder and his traditionally pro-English line, on the other. None of them, however, made any real efforts to carry through the reforms so urgently needed by now, especially in regard of taxation, which weighed heavily on the population, impeded rather than stimulated the economy, and brought the government little benefit because of the system of farming out taxes.

After the restoration of the stadholderate William IV was no keener to introduce a general reform of government. Moreover, he died young, in 1751, and his son did not come of age until 1766. William V (1748-1806) was competent and hard-working, but he showed little understanding of the growing dissatisfaction with conditions in the Republic, and he had no sympathy for the new ideas about the state and broader popular government that were being proclaimed by philosophers abroad and gaining ground in the Netherlands too.

8. Revolution and Restoration: 1780-1830

In the Northern as well as the Southern Netherlands the tensions that were to rack many European nations towards the end of the eighteenth century had been steadily growing. They reached their most violent climax in the French Revolution of 1789. In the United Provinces, opposition to William V intensified in the course of the 1780s. The so-called Patriots, however, attacked not only the stadholder but also the regent class, whose power they sought to limit. For some years it looked as if the Patriot movement was winning. William V was deprived of several offices; some town councils were modernized somewhat; the reformers created small volunteer armies. But the Orangists, with the support of England and Prussia (William V's wife Wilhelmina was a Prussian princess), launched a counter-offensive, and when in 1787 a Prussian army came to restore William V in his function as stadholder, it met virtually no resistance. From 1787 till 1795 the Republic was again ruled by the Orangist party.

In the Southern Netherlands there was resistance around this time against the policies of the emperor Joseph II, who wanted to govern his lands in a more rational and more modern way. He restricted the influence of the Church, overhauled the judicial system, and curbed the power of the provincial authorities. These measures were openly resisted from 1787 onwards. In 1789 many Austrian officials had to flee the country and an independent Belgian constitution was proclaimed (1790). But the reformers were soon divided among themselves, and when Leopold II succeeded Joseph II in 1790, he managed to restore Austrian rule by peaceful means.

In the case of both the Northern and the Southern Netherlands we can speak of a protest movement inspired by nationalism and directed against governments regarded as despotic. In both countries the movement collapsed. Shortly afterwards, however, the entire area was caught up in a revolutionary tide that engulfed France in 1789 and then swept across all of Europe. The South's fate in the period of the Revolution was utterly unlike that of the Netherlands. The country was conquered and occupied by the French in 1794, and annexed in October 1795. It underwent thorough reforms, more radical than those envisaged by Joseph II ten years before but more or less in the same spirit. The old class structure was dismantled and the influence of the Catholic Church combatted. Industrial entrepreneurs were given opportunities to set up new businesses (the Ghent textile industry, for example) and to modernize and develop existing ones (coal mining in the Borinage, textiles in Verviers) with the help of new techniques - such as steam engines - imported from England by legal or illegal means. Of great future importance was the fact that in Flanders the middle classes too now began to use French, which widened the gap separating them from the mass of peasants and workers, who continued to speak their local Dutch dialects.

In the Northern Netherlands the French period was very different. French armies overran the country in 1795, but it was not annexed until 1810 (although Napoleon had made his brother Louis king of the former republic as early as 1806). In this way the people of the Northern Netherlands, in contrast with the South, were able to modernize their own state, be it under the watchful eyes of the French. The results of the operation may be summed up in two sentences. The federal state which the Republic had been was transformed in these years into a unitary state - a political revolution of considerable significance. But the second point is that there was no social revolution of any kind. The Dutch mercantile economy suffered terrible blows as a result of French policies and the continuing war with England. As for the new industries, the Netherlands lacked raw materials like coal and iron ore which Belgium possessed, so that commercial and financial decline could not be compensated for by industrial modernization. It stands to reason that so unfavourable an economic climate did not leave much room for social improvement.

When in 1813 Napoleon was defeated by a coalition of his - by now numerous - enemies and the French withdrew from the areas they had annexed or occupied, many of their reforms were abolished as a matter of course, but nowhere was there a return to the situation as it had been before the Revolution. As regards the Low Countries, no attempt was made either in the North or in the South to restore the provincial and municipal autonomy that had been a cornerstone of the federal form of government under the *ancien régime*. On the instigation of what was in fact only a small group of leading politicians in

The Hague, the Dutch state was transformed into a monarchy as early as December 1813, with William I (1772-1843), son of stadholder William V (who had died in 1806), as the new king. But while the great powers were content to let the Dutch go about their own business, a question-mark hung over the fate of the Southern Netherlands. Austria was not keen to resume control of these rather unprofitable and distant possessions. Yet they could not be declared independent: they had never known independence before, and after nearly twenty years as an integral part of France they seemed less than ever entitled to it. The Congress of Vienna, at which the map of Europe was redrawn by the victorious powers in consultation with French representatives, decided to join the Southern and the Northern Netherlands together into a unitary state under King William I. The new state was thought to be sufficiently powerful to act as a bulwark against France, that unpredictable country that might not be prepared to curb its expansionism unless forced to do so. In other words, the Kingdom of the United Netherlands came into being in 1814 for reasons of international security: it stood as a fortress on France's northern border.

William I's realm was a constitutional monarchy. The constitution itself, though much less „democratic" than any that had been promulgated in the early days of the French Revolution, was certainly not reactionary. It acknowledged the importance of national representation in the States-General, which consisted of a Second Chamber elected by the seventeen provincial States and a First Chamber appointed by the king. It protected the individual's right to freedom and property. But it also left a great deal of power to the king, who consequently ruled the country in a rather authoritarian manner. He saw it as his prime duty to maintain two things: prosperity and unity. He succeeded in the former aim, but failed in the latter. William's economic policies undoubtedly benefitted the Southern provinces, as his personal initiatives and financial support contributed to the spread of modern industries there. But the attempt to weld the Southern and Northern provinces together on the basis of a shared sense of national identity met with little success. When Europe was going through another period of unrest in 1830, Liberal as well as Catholic politicians in Belgium managed to inspire an anti-Dutch, anti-Protestant and finally anti-Orangist movement. William I appeared to have no adequate defence, and the proud new kingdom fell apart. In 1831 the great powers recognized the independence of a separate Belgian state, which soon acquired its own king, Leopold I (1790-1865) of Saxe-Coburg.

9. Two National States: 1830-1880

The Southern Netherlands had never constituted an independent state, so that Belgium was a new creation. However, in the view of its architects and founders, the Belgian nation, far from being new, had an ancient lineage, and they regarded it as entirely consistent with the spirit of history that it should now have been given its own political identity. A consensus was soon reached on the form the new state should take, and in 1831 the new constitution was framed, creating a modern parliamentary monarchy, a unitary state with a Chamber of Representatives directly elected by a (limited) number of voters, and a Senate for the upper classes. But although this ensured that ultimate political power resided with parliament and the cabinet, and the monarchical principle which had prevailed under William I was abolished, the sovereign was nevertheless allowed ample room for manœuvre, and accordingly was able to continue to exert considerable political influence in Belgium far into the twentieth century. While it had been relatively easy to reach agreement on the constitution itself, conflicts soon arose over the question whether the nation which had assumed this form was basically a traditional Catholic community, or rather a progressive bourgeois society, striving for modernization, intellectual freedom, economic expansion, urbanization and secularization. In other words, Catholic and

William I entering Brussels as King of the United Netherlands, 1815 (aquatint by P.L. Debucourt).

Liberal opinion was once again clearly polarized, as it had been in previous periods of the country's history. In 1830, however, the advocates of Liberal principles had been able to work together with Catholic leaders, because of their shared opposition to the policies of William I, albeit on different grounds. Once Belgium had become independent, the basis of their co-operation was removed and their diametrically opposed points of view re-emerged. Until the late 1840s the Catholics retained the upper hand, as was most clearly apparent from the Primary Education Act of 1842, which gave the clergy some say in state education. In 1846, partly in response to this, a well-attended congress of Liberal supporters assembled and formulated a concrete political programme. This was a watershed, since it meant that Liberal opinion was now focussed in a modern political party of the kind we know today. It was to be a considerable time before Belgian Catholics followed their example: not until the 1860s did a comparable organization emerge from within their ranks. In the Netherlands there was no question of such a modern process of party formation until 1878.

From 1847 until 1884 Belgium was ruled predominantly by the Liberals, led at first by Charles Rogier (1800-1885), who had been one of the leaders of the 1830 Revolution, and subsequently by H.J.W. Frère-Orban (1812-1896). The Liberals' chief concerns were the economy and education. The Belgian economy was growing rapidly. The first stirrings of the so-called „Industrial Revolution" dated from the early years of the nineteenth century, but the process was not completed until the 1840s, making Belgium the first country in mainland Europe to have built up a modern heavy industry, based in Wallonia. In the nineteenth century, in contrast to the Medieval heyday of the Southern Netherlands, it was the French-speaking provinces which were the most highly-developed and prosperous, while Flanders was undergoing a serious crisis. However, at this time the economy was not yet the object of full-scale political debate, unlike education, on which Catholics and Liberals were on several occasions locked in fierce conflict, in 1850 about secondary education, and in 1879 on primary schooling. On both occasions the anti-clerical Liberals won the day, with the result that the influence of the clergy on state schools became minimal. The Church, however, refused to concede defeat, and in a subsequent period succeeded in overturning some Liberal gains.

The opposition between Liberals and Catholics was regarded at this time as much more important than that between Walloons and Flemings. In Flanders as well as in Wallonia the ruling middle classes were French-speaking. Similarly, the Church did not attach great significance to the language problem. The bishops were French-speaking, and while the lesser clergy in Flanders of course spoke Dutch and were sometimes openly pro-Flemish, they were given no opportunity by the bishops to make their resistance to the hegemony of French a more forceful one, and the mass of the Flemish population remained fairly passive. Nevertheless, during the 1870s and early 1880s some legislation was passed which went some way towards strengthening the position of Dutch in jurisprudence, administration and secondary education. Its implementation, however, left much to be desired, and so inequities persisted: some two million Dutch-speakers were governed and stood trial in a language they could not understand.

The development of the Netherlands in the period up to 1880 took a different course from that of Belgium. Its economy was not, until the 1890s, modernized to the same extent. This meant that Belgium, which at the time of separation in 1830 had undoubtedly been poorer than the Netherlands, was able in the succeeding half century to catch up. By 1880, even without rich colonies - thanks to the so-called „Culture System", introduced in 1830, the Netherlands derived vast income from the Dutch East Indies through compulsorily grown cash crops such as coffee, sugar and indigo marketed through a government monopoly - it was certainly no longer economically inferior to its northern neighbour. Whereas Belgium produced a Liberal constitution as early as 1831, the Netherlands waited until 1848. Moreover, the modern political parties which were forming in Belgium at this time were unknown in the Netherlands. Yet in spite of this there are also clear parallels. From mid-century onwards, politics in both countries were overwhelmingly Liberal in complexion, which means that the modernization which occurred in both nations, albeit at different rates and in differing degrees, was stimulated and achieved by Liberals. This continued to influence the nature of both countries even when Liberal dominance was undermined at the end of the century.

In the fifty years after 1830 the Netherlands produced several important historians, essayists and novelists, as well as a number of statesmen of stature, principal among them Johan Rudolf Thorbecke (1798-1872), the architect of the Liberal constitution of 1848. Foremost among the high-quality newspapers and journals founded during the period was *De Gids* (The Guide), a political and cultural monthly which first appeared in 1837. In the second half of the century, the painting of the so-called Hague School attracted international attention. From the 1830s and 1840s onwards Dutch culture in its broadest sense assumed a more modern character than in the early nineteenth and eighteenth centuries and the country adapted with some relish to its new status. For it must be borne in mind that when the Dutch state achieved independence at the end of the sixteenth century, its economic strength soon gave it the status of a great power. Even in the eighteenth century the Republic, for all its weakness, continued to be regarded as a force to be reckoned with, albeit one in decline. From 1815 to 1830 the United Netherlands counted as a medium-sized power. After Belgium's secession from this union in 1830, the Kingdom of the Netherlands was left to its own devices, having become, for the first time in its history, nothing more than a minor state, undoubtedly ranking somewhat ahead of Belgium on the strength of its great colonies, but nevertheless not essentially different from its southern neighbour. The Netherlands found themselves in an entirely new situation. No-one could ever have foreseen that from the middle of the nineteenth century onwards the delta of the great European rivers would be controlled by two small, neutral, constitutional monarchies, economically highly-developed, militarily weak, politically stable and with modest aspirations.

10. A Flourishing Period: 1880-1914

From 1880 onwards the nature of society in both Belgium and the Netherlands changed gradually, but at the same time quite radically. The population grew, in Belgium from 4.3 million in 1846 to 7.6 million in 1913; in the Netherlands from 3 to 6 million. After 1890 the Netherlands too entered the modern industrial era and an industrial proletariat of some size began to emerge. In the 1880s a Socialist party was founded, but remained quite weak. The Social-Democratic Workers' Party (SDAP), set up in 1894, was more successful, and in the form it assumed in 1946, the Labour Party (Partij van de Arbeid) is still going strong. In the Dutch East Indies after 1870 more scope was given to private enterprise than in preceding decades, but at the same time Dutch authority spread far wider through the Indonesian archipelago than ever before. From 1900 onwards the Dutch government began to spend more on developing the colony; it improved the infrastructure, devoted more attention to education and social welfare, and felt itself obliged, as a conscientious guardian, to educate its ward to the point where it could control its own affairs (though this, in its view, would be a very long process).

In the home country itself male suffrage was greatly extended in 1887 and 1896, primary schooling became compulsory in 1900, and the incomes of the middle classes were at last (from 1892) directly taxed, so that state revenues increased and certain indirect taxes, which were a particularly heavy burden on the lower classes, could be abolished or reduced. The 1880s also saw the beginnings of social legislation which afforded workers, women and children some measure of protection against the effects of the free market. One can therefore observe all kinds of innovations, which were to be greatly extended in the twentieth century. Among these is the emergence of the system of polarized interest groups within the country, which was later to become known in Dutch as „verzuiling" (lit. „pillarization"). Because of the opportunities gained by the Calvinists and Roman Catholics during this period to use state assistance to set up their own primary, secondary and even higher education, as well as special social welfare programmes for their co-religionists (in the form of sickness insurance, hospitals, and all manner of societies and trades unions), they were able to construct around their political parties (which were founded at this time) an ever-expanding network of organizations on which large numbers of people came to depend. As a result the various groups within the population began to isolate themselves from each other to some extent within their own „pillar", and even the non-denominational parties, especially the Socialists, were soon forced to try to construct something similar. In this way Protestant, Catholic, Socialist and arguably even Liberal pillars arose, whose joint function was seen as supporting the roof of Dutch society.

Belgium operated a similar system. The Catholics were given the opportunity to construct not only their own system of education, but also an extensive complex of social, medical and cultural provision. The Socialists followed their example, albeit on a more modest scale, and the end-result was that in Belgium too countless citizens relied for their needs in these areas on their own organizations. As in the Netherlands, this increased the importance of the political parties, which had the task of ensuring the provision of sufficient state funds to their social organizations. To a greater extent than in the Netherlands, however, Belgian society became so politicized as a result of this situation that many civil service appointments effectively required the approval of the political parties, thus undermining the principle that in a modern state the bureaucracy should be neutral and impartial.

Belgian history is characterized at this period by colonial involvement, the rise of Socialism, a degree of democratization, and - a specifically Belgian problem - the exacerbation of the divisions between Flemings and Walloons. Belgium owed its one colony to King Leopold II (1835-1909), who succeeded his father in 1865. He created a country, the Congo, out of an area of Central Africa only recently „discovered" by the white man, which in 1885 was conditionally recognized by the Great Powers as a sovereign state ruled by him. From about 1895 onwards Leopold's kingdom began to yield rich profits (derived mostly from rubber), partly as a result of the ruthless policies adopted by Leopold in respect of the native population. This provoked strong protests, especially from British and American quarters, and in 1908 the king was forced to hand over his private colony to the Belgian state. Belgium thus became a colonial power and remained so until 1960.

When one considers that Belgium was the first country in Europe to experience the Industrial Revolution and hence already had a sizeable industrial proletariat, the late appearance of Socialism is striking. However, after its foundation in 1885 the Belgian Workers' Party (Belgische Werklieden Partij, Parti Ouvrier Belge) grew rapidly. When, following violent demonstrations and a concerted campaign, universal (male) suffrage was introduced in 1893 but the better educated members of society nevertheless retained their privileged position by virtue of the so-called „plural vote", the BWP scored considerable electoral successes. However, it did not play a part in government, and from 1884 to 1917 Belgium was ruled by a series of solidly Catholic cabinets. These made a start on the introduction of social legislation, carried through the electoral reform, and resolved the problem of Leopold's Congo State. Their support came more from Flanders than from Wallonia and it is consequently understandable that the Catholics should have shown more respect for Flemish demands than did the Liberals, who had had such great political influence in the preceding period. An additional factor was that Flanders' economic situation was beginning to improve; there were even grounds for suspecting that economic predominance in the country, which since the first phase of industrialization had rested with Wallonia, with its deposits of iron ore and coal, would in the long run once again (as in the past) revert to Flanders, with its harbours and the new industries which had been set up there.

The position of Dutch improved; in 1898 the language was given official equality with French, which meant that the Dutch version of Acts of Parliament would henceforth have the same force in law as the French. In the field of education too, the Flemish Movement gained ground: not only in the primary sector, but also in the secondary schools, both Catholic and state-run, Dutch was increasingly used as the medium of instruction. The University of Ghent (originally founded by William I), which immediately after the Belgian Revolution had opted for French, and the Catholic University of Louvain (re-established 1834), still only admitted the use of Dutch in very restricted fields. The Flemish Movement was not able to convince Belgian politicians that the intellectual elite need not be by definition French-speaking. This was of course not the case in the Netherlands, and although the French-speaking Flemish writers Emile Verhaeren and Maurice Maeterlinck gained worldwide celebrity of a kind denied to Dutch-language authors from either the South (like August Vermeylen) or the North (like the great poet Herman Gorter), in the natural sciences it was precisely Dutch research that gained great international recognition, as is evidenced by the Nobel Prizes it was awarded. In both countries the period from 1880 to 1914 witnessed a remarkable cultural flowering.

11. 1914-1945

The Low Countries became caught up against their will in the European War, which spanned thirty years and assumed global proportions - Belgium as early as 1914, the Netherlands only in 1940. They were victims and were forced to participate in a process which they had tried to keep beyond their borders. In August 1914 German troops invaded Belgium. Since their main object was to cut a path into France, there was a delay before they found time to conquer Belgium in its entirety. In fact, a strip of strategically important land to the west of the River IJzer remained unconquered throughout the war, and it

The Clothmakers' Hall at Ypres in ruïns (1916).

was here that King Albert set up his headquarters. Belgium suffered heavily under German occupation, particularly in a material sense. After the military engagements of the summer and autumn of 1914 were over and the German campaign of terror against the civilian population during the first period of conflict had petered out, personal losses were limited in scale. But it has been calculated that as a result of German actions Belgium suffered losses to the tune of between six and seven billion francs (at 1913 value), in other words some 12 % of its pre-war wealth, and after the war received no more than two billion francs in reparation. The political damage was also considerable. During the occupation a number of Flemish militants tried to exploit the situation to gain Flemish autonomy. With German help a Dutch-language university was set up in Ghent, and in 1917 the Germans, pressured by these so-called „activists", divided the unitary state of Belgium into Dutch-speaking and French-speaking halves. Naturally these actions of the activists caused much resentment after Germany's defeat, and the struggle for Flemish „emancipation" suffered a serious setback.

The Netherlands was spared by the German armies in 1914 and was able to stay neutral for the duration of the war. Initially this was to its economic advantage, later not. But it did not suffer any great losses and was able to prepare for democracy in comparative calm: in 1917 universal male suffrage was finally introduced (followed shortly afterwards by female suffrage). The result was that from then until 1940 the country was ruled by governments in which the Catholic and Protestant parties were dominant. The Socialists remained in opposition until 1939. In 1919 Belgium abolished the electoral system which had operated since 1893 and introduced single-vote male suffrage (women were not to be given the vote until 1948). In contrast to the Netherlands, the Socialist party did form part of various governments during this period. In many ways the interwar period was a more difficult one for Belgium than for the Netherlands. It took until about 1925 before it had recovered from its wartime losses and by the beginning of the 1930s the repercussions of the 1929 Wall Street stockmarket crash were painfully in evidence. Nevertheless, there is no doubt that poverty declined overall during the interwar years, thanks to the rise in the level of affluence and to the improvement in the provision of social welfare. But human economic misery had not been done away with for good and as a result of the Depression threatened to grow once again to unmanageable proportions.

Even the active foreign policy on which Belgium - which from 1839 until 1914 had been officially neutral - embarked after 1918 led to nothing but disappointment and confusion. The attempts made in the immediate aftermath of the First World War to acquire, with the help of the Great Powers, Dutch territory in Limburg and Zeeland-Flanders, marred relations with the Netherlands and produced only friction and loss of face. Attempts to strengthen the international position of the country with French help did not in the event increase Belgian prestige. In 1936 Belgium abandoned these activities, but the neutrality which it redeclared in that year was breached by Germany in May 1940. The intractable Flemish-Walloon problem remained unresolved, though the Flemish Movement, whose freedom of action had been seriously limited during the 1920s because of the abortive wartime escapades of the activists, had some successes during the 1930s. One of the most important of these was without doubt the final creation of a Dutch-language university at Ghent (which in 1918 had reverted to French as its medium of instruction), thus making it possible for Dutch-speakers to be educated entirely in their own language. The Catholic University of Louvain did not go as far, but did at least place Dutch on an equal footing with French.

On 28 June 1932 an Act emphatically stating the principle that Flanders was Dutch-speaking - that is, not bilingual but monolingual - became law, and was backed up by the introduction of measures against any breach of its terms. On 14 July 1932 a Primary and Secondary Education Act was passed making the use of Dutch in teaching compulsory both in state schools and in other, mostly Catholic institutions. In 1935 it was decreed that (with a few exceptions) all legal cases in Flanders were to be conducted exclusively in Dutch. Certainly, it was to take some time before the establishment of Flanders as a Dutch-language area became a social reality, but there was no longer any doubt that the process would rapidly be concluded.

The Netherlands had an easier time of it, despite the fact that it certainly suffered severely from the Depression of the 1930s, during which hundreds of thousands of unemployed were for years forced to resign themselves to a bleak and impoverished existence. It is, however, worthy of note that neither in Belgium nor in the Netherlands did the Fascist and National-Socialist parties which were set up in order to combat the crisis in the same way Hitler was tackling it in Germany, enjoy much success. The primarily French-speaking Rexist movement and the Flemish National Alliance (Vlaams Nationaal Verbond) in Belgium, and the Dutch National-Socialist Movement (NSB), though they attracted a good deal of attention during the 1930s and at times appeared to have considerable support, never achieved the status of mass movements, and their support waned rather than increased shortly before the Second World War. When the Germans invaded the Low Countries in May 1940, they did not find large groups of people who supported their aims: they found rather well-disciplined, quite calm and stable populations, the vast majority of which, despite the disappointments of the interwar years, rejected Nazi revolutionary philosophies and were utterly hostile to Germany's plan to absorb them into the Pan-German Reich.

The occupation of Belgium, which lasted from May 1940 until August 1944, caused less damage proportionally (8 % of

Emmy Andriesse, „Child with a small saucepan". During the winter of 1944-45 there were serious food shortages in the western Netherlands.

its national wealth in 1939) than German occupation during the First World War. However, the cost in human life was greater (more than 50,000 dead), and the political and moral aftermath was worse for the post-war generation. The Netherlands, which was partially liberated in August 1944, but not completely until May 1945, was much worse off: both material losses (33 % of its 1939 GNP) and personal suffering were four times those in Belgium. Whilst the Belgium of 1944, though of course economically weaker than it had been in 1940, was definitely not a shattered country, the Netherlands of 1945 certainly was, and was in addition racked by the guilt which even in the view of its most fervent advocates it had incurred by looking passively on while the Germans deported and murdered almost the entire Jewish population (some 90,000 people in all).

It took some years after 1945 before both countries came to terms with the legacy of the war. Many tens of thousands of people suspected of collaboration with the occupying forces were tried and punished, though only a relatively small number were sentenced to death. King Leopold III (1901-1985), unlike the Dutch monarch, Queen Wilhelmina, who had gone into exile in London, had remained in his country. In the view of his critics he had shown himself far too accommodating, and in 1950 he realized, after a long and acrimonious controversy, that there was no alternative for him but to abdicate. Only then was Belgian political life able to return to normal.

12. 1945-1980

The war did little to alter the domestic situation in either country. The old political parties returned under new names; social structures remained basically unchanged. Social legislation was, however, considerably improved and workers and those in employment generally gained greater opportunities to protect their interests. Partly because of this they were able from the outset to partake in the astonishing economic recovery which Europe experienced in the 1950s and which in the Benelux countries as elsewhere soon raised the level of prosperity to hitherto unprecedented heights. It is incidentally worthy of note that in the Netherlands, which had been harder hit by the war, economic recovery went hand in hand with economic and technological renewal of a kind absent from Belgium in the initial period. The Netherlands experienced the twentieth-century Industrial Revolution before Belgium (which is interesting, since in the case of the original one it had lagged half a century behind).

The countries' place in international politics altered dramatically. Their neutrality had been of no help to them in 1940, which led to a rethinking of their foreign policy after 1945. Even during the war - thanks in large measure to the efforts of the Belgian Foreign Minister, Paul-Henri Spaak (1899-1972) - discussions had been held on closer co-operation between Belgium, the Netherlands and Luxemburg, which led to the Benelux Customs Union of 1948 and in 1958 to the Benelux Economic Union. The Benelux - that is, an alliance of three states which prior to 1940 had taken a strictly neutral stance - had a major share in the realization of the 1949 NATO treaty and in 1958 in the creation of the European Economic Community.

At the same time that they abandoned the political isolationism into which they had withdrawn in the nineteenth and early twentieth centuries, both Belgium and the Netherlands were forced to relinquish the colonial empires which in the past had quite significantly boosted their international status and economic prosperity. In 1949, after years of prognostication and conflict, the Dutch yielded to the pressure exerted by the Great Powers and recognized the independence of the Republic of Indonesia. When ten years later the wave of decolonialization overtook Africa, the Belgians hastily abandoned their colony in the Congo (1960), which soon afterwards became the present-day Zaire. Since 1831 Belgium had been a unitary constitutional monarchy, with a population somewhat larger than that of the Netherlands, and with a more rapidly developing economy, but after it began to assume the status of a colonial power in the 1880s through the agency of its king, it became more comparable with its neighbour than ever before. In 1960 it once again suffered a similar fate to the Netherlands. As a result of the postwar population explosion in the Netherlands, it had become somewhat less populous (in 1960, Belgium had 9,200,000 inhabitants, compared with the Netherlands' 11,556,000), and was economically less up to date in its infrastructure, but the two countries were obviously closely related as regards both their structure and their position in the world.

There was, however, one basic difference, which was particularly highlighted in the 1960s and 1970s. Since the late eighteenth century the Netherlands had been in all of its various manifestations a national state, and so it remained. Belgium had been founded in 1831 as a national state, but did not remain one. Throughout the 1960s, a period in which the Low Countries shared the general growth in prosperity, the non-national character of Belgium became clearly and poignantly apparent. One of the reasons why the divisions between French- and Dutch-speakers received so much emphasis precisely at this time, is an economic one: the Flemish provinces benefitted far more from the modernization of the economy, foreign investment and growing employment opportunities than did Wallonia, with its ageing industry, based on worked-out coalmines, which were anyway no longer viable, given the enormous increase in the use of alternative energy sources such as oil and gas. The industrial centre of gravity in Belgium shifted to Flanders, which was now more populous, energetic and powerful. This led both Walloons, who felt themselves disadvantaged, and Flemings, who were not disposed to support Wallonia financially, to argue for a radical reform of the Belgian state. Conditions seemed propitious: in a period like the 1960s, when both at home and abroad so many received notions - on religion, morality, patriotism, property, etc. - were suddenly being questioned, and new experiments could apparently be amply funded from the proceeds of unparalleled prosperity, it became almost inevitable that the unitary state of Belgium should be finally transformed into a semi-federal state, whose constituent parts would enjoy a degree of autonomy. An attempt was made to give this new conception concrete form by constitutional reforms (in 1970 and 1980), but with only very partial success. The country's constitutional structure has become extremely complex, and may soon have to be changed yet again. But it is clear that Belgium can never again be a national state, and that if it is able to weather the storm, will demonstrate the falsehood of the widely-held twentieth-century view that the modern state must be national if it is to survive.

The Netherlands and Belgium did not emerge into nationhood through some natural, organic historical process. Their history is a complex one, and if one looks back at it from today's vantage-point it can often seem confused, full of question marks, ambiguities and totally unexpected leaps in the dark. But it is at the same time impressive, in that for all its arbitrariness it demonstrates the vitality and inventiveness of the peoples who have inhabited this part of Europe. At some point these countries or states will of course disappear from history in their turn. It is to be hoped that they will be praised in posterity's funeral orations for their undeniable merit as thoroughly civilized communities, with a strange but rich historical heritage.

843 Treaty of Verdun, the first of a series of treaties dividing up the Carolingian Empire.

1363-1482 „Burgundian Period"; the Dukes of Burgundy gradually take over the greater part of the Low Countries.

1477 Charles the Bold, Duke of Burgundy, killed at the Battle of Nancy. His daughter and heir Mary (d.1482) marries Maximilian of Habsburg.

1500-1555 Charles V inherits the Habsburg Netherlands, Spain and its colonies, and becomes German Emperor.

1555 Philip II succeeds Charles V. His policies provoke resentment and open opposition.

1566 Iconoclastic Riots spread from South-West Flanders: Calvinist groups seize church buildings, break the images and remove Roman Catholic liturgical objects.

1568-1572 First phase of the Revolt of the Netherlands. Egmond and Horne beheaded. First military confrontation.

1576 Pacification of Ghent. The Southern and Northern provinces agree on joint resistance to the policies of Philip II.

1579 Union of Arras. Hainaut and Artois submit to the authority of Philip II and the Roman Catholic Church. Union of Utrecht: alliance of the rebel territories.

1581 Edict of Abjuration: the rebel territories cease to recognize Philip as their rightful sovereign.

1584 William the Silent, Prince of Orange, leader of the resistance against Philip II, assassinated at Delft.

1585 Fall of Antwerp and closure of the Scheldt estuary.

1588 Beginning of consolidation of the Republic of the Seven United Provinces of the Netherlands.

1598-1621 Rule of Archduke Albrecht and Archduchess Isabella in the southern Netherlands (1609-1621: Twelve Years' Truce).

1648 Peace of Munster. The Republic recognized as an independent state. Territorial boundaries determined by *status quo*.

1650-1672 First Stadholderless Period in the Republic, ended after French invasion, when William III becomes stadholder.

1701-1714 War of the Spanish Succession. Southern Netherlands henceforth under Austrian Habsburg rule.

1740-1748 War of the Austrian Succession, abortive attempt by France to annex the Southern Netherlands.

1795 Belgium, overrun in 1794, annexed by France. The Republic, defeated by France, adopts a new constitution, but in 1810 is annexed to France by Napoleon.

1813 Fall of Napoleon. The Northern Netherlands become a monarchy: stadholder William VI becomes first sovereign prince, afterwards (in 1814) King William I.

1815-1830 (United) Kingdom of the Netherlands.

1830 Belgian Revolution.

1831 First Belgian constitution. Leopold I becomes King of the Belgians (Belgian independence recognized by the Netherlands in 1839).

1848 Thorbecke's constitutional reform in the Netherlands.

1893 Constitutional reform in Belgium: universal „plural-vote" male suffrage.

1914-1918 Greater part of Belgium occupied by Germans. The Netherlands remain neutral.

1917 Constitutional reform in the Netherlands introduces universal male suffrage (universal female suffrage granted in 1922). In 1919 universal „single-vote" male suffrage adopted in Belgium.

1940-1944/45 Belgium and the Netherlands under German occupation.

1947 Benelux Treaty between Belgium, the Netherlands and Luxemburg.

1970, 1980 Constitutional reforms in Belgium redefine the position of Flanders, Wallonia and Brussels.

14. Recommended for further reading

BLOK, P.J. *History of the People of the Netherlands,* London, 1898-1912. Reprint: New York, 1970.

BOXER, C.R., *The Dutch Seaborne Empire,* London, 1965.

CARSON, PATRICIA, *The Fair Face of Flanders,* Ghent, 1969.

CLOUGH, S.B., *A History of the Flemish Movement in Belgium,* New York, 1930. Reprint: 1968.

DIJKSTERHUIS, E.J. *Simon Stevin. Science in the Netherlands around 1600,* The Hague, 1970.

FITZMAURICE, J., *The Politics of Belgium. Crisis and Compromise in a Plural Society,* London, 1983.

GEYL, P., *The Revolt of the Netherlands, 1559-1609,* London, 1958.

GEYL, P., *The Netherlands of the Seventeenth Century,* 2 vols., London, 1961-1964.

GEYL, P., *History of the Low Countries: Episodes and Problems,* London, 1964.

GUTMAN, M.P., *War und Rural Life in the Early Modern Low Countries,* Assen, 1980.

HALEY, K.H., *The Dutch in the Seventeenth Century,* London, 1972.

HOUTTE, J.A. VAN, *An Economic History of the Low Countries, 800-1800,* London, 1977.

HUIZINGA, J., *Dutch Civilization in the Seventeenth Century,* London, 1968.

KOSSMANN, E.H., *The Low Countries 1780-1940,* Oxford, 1978.

LEEB, J.L., *The Ideological Origins of the Batavian Revolution. History and Politics in the Dutch Republic 1747-1800,* The Hague, 1977.

LINDEN, H. VAN DER, *Belgium, the Making of a Nation,* Oxford, 1920.

MOKYR, J., *Industrialization in the Low Countries 1795-1850,* New Haven, 1975.

NEWTON, G., *The Netherlands: A Historical and Cultural Survey, 1795-1977.* London/Boulder, 1978.

NICHOLAS, D.M., *Town and Countryside: Social, Economic and Political Tensions in Fourteenth-Century Flanders,* Bruges, 1971.

PARKER, G., *The Army of Flanders and the Spanish Road,* Cambridge, 1972.

PRICE, J.L., *Culture and Society in the Dutch Republic during the Seventeenth Century,* London, 1974.

RENIER, G., *The Dutch Nation,* London, 1944.

ROWEN, H.H., *John de Witt, Grand Pensionary of Holland 1625-1672,* Princeton, 1978.

SCHAMA, S., *Patriots and Liberators. Revolution in the Netherlands, 1780-1813,* New York, 1971.

TEX., J. DEN, *Oldenbarnevelt,* 2 vols., Cambridge, 1973.

VAUGHAN, R., *Valois Burgundy,* London, 1975.

VRIES, J. DE., *The Netherlands Economy in the Twentieth Century: an Examination of the Most Characteristic Features in the Period 1900-1970,* Assen, 1978.

WEDGWOOD, C.V., *William the Silent,* London, 1944.

WILSON, C., *Profit and Power. A Study of England and the Dutch Wars,* London, 1957.

WILSON, C., *The Dutch Republic and the Civilisation of the Seventeenth Century,* London, 1968

In Dutch:

Algemene geschiedenis der Nederlanden, ed. J.A. van Houtte et al.; 15 vols., Utrecht, 1977-1982.

Contents